IMAGES OF ENGLAND

BIRMINGHAM
BETWEEN THE WARS

IMAGES OF ENGLAND

BIRMINGHAM
BETWEEN THE WARS

ERIC ARMSTRONG

TEMPUS

Frontispiece: An interesting corner of bygone Handsworth where the Crompton Road post office is advertised in Church Hill Road. Postal services were provided from within a new ladies' dress shop opened adjacent to the corner shop. Adjoining this dress shop stood the wonderful newsagents of Mr F.W. Baker. The fanlight above the grocer advertises Eiffel Tower Lemonade. According to a 1931 magazine, '50 Million Lemons' a year were used to make the drink. In the left-hand window of the grocer's shop is advertised 'Drew's Self Raising Flour'.

First published 2004

Tempus Publishing Limited
The Mill, Brimscombe Port,
Stroud, Gloucestershire, GL5 2QG
www.tempus-publishing.com

British Library Cataloguing in Publication Data.
A catalogue record for this book is available from the British Library.

ISBN 0 7524 3145 5

Typesetting and origination by Tempus Publishing Limited.
Printed in Great Britain by Midway Colour Print, Wiltshire.

Contents

Grosvenor Road, Handsworth, Birmingham. Drew's Mill was a familiar local landmark. If you were travelling on the outer circle bus along Wellington Road (from the direction of Perry Barr) and wanted to alight near The Calthorpe Arms, then it was time to get to your feet when Drew's Mill came into view.

Acknowledgements

In carrying out the research required for this book I warmly acknowledge the help I have received from the following sources:

Deighton, Len, & Arnold Schwartzman, *Airshipwreck*, Book Club Associates by arrangement with Jonathan Cape Ltd, 1978
Dudley Archives and Local History Service
Her Majesty's Stationery Office
Marks, John, *Birmingham on Old Postcards: Reflections of a Bygone Age*, Vol. 1, 1982; Vol. 2 1983; Vol. 3 1990)
Street, Sean, A., *Concise History of British Radio 1922-2002*, Kelly Publications, 2002
This England's Book of British Dance Bands from the Twenties to the Fifties, This England Books, 1999
This England's Second Book of British Dance Bands, The Singers and smaller bands This England Books, 2001

For the use of copyright material the author is particularly grateful to:
Mirror Pix
D.C. Thomson & Co. Ltd

Introduction

'Between the wars' signifies a period of peace which prevailed from 11 November 1918 to 3 September 1939. Yet, although not at war during the 1920s and for most of the 1930s, Britain was self-evidently not at peace with itself during those years. In fact, a great deal of economic, social and political turbulence occurred during the two decades under review.

Realisation soon grew that the 'war to end all wars', the Great War of 1914–18, was probably an illusion, despite the founding of the forerunner to the United Nations, namely the League of Nations in 1919. The land 'fit for heroes', newly returned from the trenches, did not materialise. Ex-servicemen, with many wounded among them, hawking matches and bootlaces from trays to earn a pittance, became an all too common and shaming sight on city streets.

As mass unemployment grew so did mass protest culminating in the General Strike of 1926 and, in symbolic terms, the Jarrow Hunger March of 1936. State attempts to alleviate poverty by the dole remained feeble and the control of financial support by 'the means test' was widely reviled. Support grew for the extremes of the political spectrum, i.e. fascism and communism. Even at school, formal debate about the Spanish Civil War and foreign intervention provoked genuinely bitter exchanges.

By one of history's grim ironies, Britain began to claw its way out of economic depression by starting a contentious programme of rearmament. While many people remained opposed to war, general public opinion began to shift to the position that Britain should be capable of defending itself and its Empire against the threats posed by Italian, Russian and especially German dictatorships. Just a year after the 'peace for our time' agreement of 1938, Britain went to war, not as in 1914, in a jingoistic, 'we'll be home for Christmas' spirit but rather in a mood to hold out against totalitarianism and hopefully defeat it.

In brief, it can be said with a reasonable measure of accuracy that the 1920s were characterised by trying to come to terms with the Great War's horrific legacy while accepting that what later came to be called World War Two was inevitable if Britain was to survive in anything like its traditional form.

The very broad summary above has inevitably been influenced by hindsight and the maturity of age. It also needs to be said that whatever period of history is under review, the beginning of that period can be better understood if its immediate past is given some attention, as has been done in this book. For similar reasons of continuity, the first year or so of war following the end of peace in September 1939 throws into sharper relief the character of the inter-war years, as experienced by one young Brummie.

So, what was it really like to grow up during those years of peace? This book, if only briefly, seeks to answer that question principally in a pictorial form by presenting, with comments, nostalgic documents of three main kinds: broadly contemporary postcards, photographs from the family album, and illustrations and excerpts from a variety of ephemera sources including cigarette cards, magazines, school examination papers, advertisements and personal diaries. While no claim is made that this particular 'boy's view' is fully representative of boys' lives of the time, I am reasonably confident that it is typical of many in Birmingham – and perhaps a fair number beyond the city's boundaries.

Quite properly, readers of all ages are likely to make comparisons between the 1920s and 1930s and the present day. Some among them, especially the younger ones, may be surprised, astonished even, at particular features of a bygone age. For example, consider the 'ancient' currency of seventy years ago.

During the 1930s a boy's weekly paper, *The Hotspur* perhaps or *The Magnet* (featuring Billy Bunter) cost two pence, i.e. eight farthings. So a pound note, (there was no pound coin), constituted the equivalent of 960 farthings! Given the size and weight of halfpenny and penny coins, it was small wonder that boys, usually in short trousers, when lucky enough to have a few coppers, would often require repairs to their trouser pockets.

It was not just a question of weight but the frequent jolting collisions of coins with other items in the pocket. Typically these might well include the almost obligatory penknife, an over twanged Jew's harp perhaps, a couple of favourite glass marbles, a tried and trusted conker, a stub of indelible pencil, a broken-off wheel from a Dinky-type toy car and a short piece of frayed string. These were all treasured possessions, some with totemic significance. Has a PhD thesis ever been written entitled, 'The contents of a schoolboy's pockets as an indicator of social and economic class?'

Of course, other indicators could be used to serve similar research purposes. Take, for example, the practices of courtesy and courtship of the 1920s and 1930s to serve as a contrast to contemporary social behaviour.

In 1930 a man typically wearing a trilby or bowler hat would, on meeting a lady acquaintance, neighbour, relative or friend in the street, raise his hat to the lady in polite greeting. Some cloth capped workers would touch the peaks of their flat caps and growl a gruff 'nice day missis' (see p.39).

'Walking out' with a girl could be followed by 'going steady' or 'courting seriously' before marriage occurred. When escorting a girl to the pictures her young man would walk nearer the edge of the pavement as a form of chivalrous protection. He would open doors to allow her to pass through into the church, the cinema or dance hall. He would often be rewarded with a charming smile.

Those brief descriptions are not to be thought of as implying criticism of present-day behaviour. They are simply illustrative of the differences between then and now. Many more are to be pointed out in this book!

Here, wherever possible, captions are written to place the pictures in as meaningful a context as space will allow, and with relevance to boyhood days. Admittedly, memories are unlikely to be of laser-like accuracy and sharpness. Even so, supportive evidence is provided by a variety of authentic documentation. For example, copies of the '11 plus' examination papers of 1934 are included. Excerpts from schoolboy diaries for 1938, 1939, and 1940 are also provided. The diaries reveal not only a critique of family and schoolboy life of sixty plus years ago but of films and sport, the mass evacuation of schoolchildren in 1939 and, best of all perhaps, an account of young love.

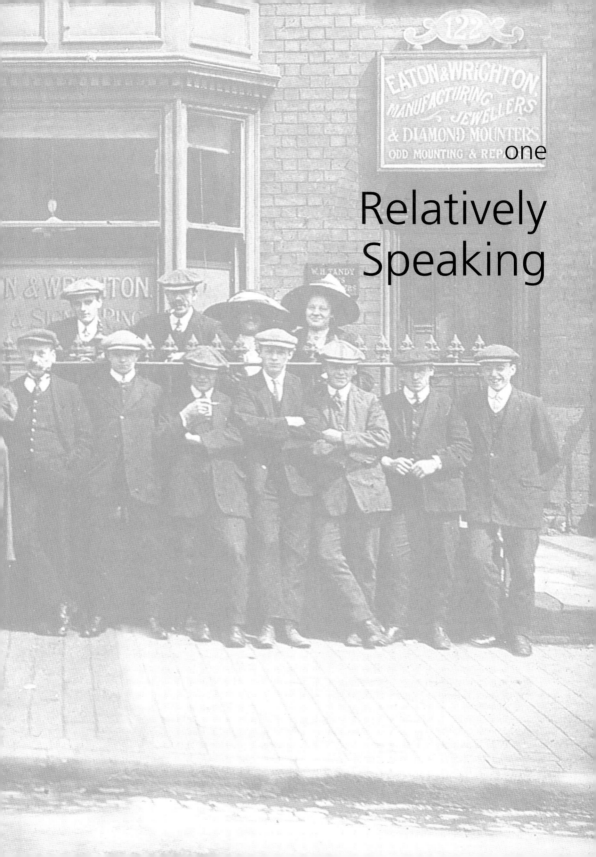

Relatively Speaking

My father, Alfred John Armstrong (1878–1965), foreground left, at work as a gem setter in Birmingham's Jewellery Quarter. Just visible is the special concave bench of the jewellery worker with its hanging leather pouch designed to catch precious metal 'waste'.

Before the First World War, my father worked regularly for Eaton and Wrighton, 'Manufacturing Jewellers & Diamond Mounters' as stated above the door. This group photograph may mark the start of the works' annual day's outing. Identified by a cross above his cap, my father is apparently wearing knickerbockers for he was a keen cyclist until illness struck. Only one man wears a bowler hat, a symbol perhaps of management status.

Left: Champion school running team, Westminster Road School, Handsworth, 1912. The eldest of my four half-brothers, Harold (1898-1918), is seated on the left. The other members of this victorious team representing the school are, clockwise; Coxon, Finchett and Constantine. The handsome shield rests against the knees of headmaster Mr Mullins. Mr Jones is the other teacher standing at the back of this picture.

Right: Harold served as a gunner in the Royal Field Artillery. On 15 September 1918 his battery commander wrote to my father, 'your son … was killed outright … doing runner at the time between Brigade and the Battery, all telephone wires having been cut … The duties of runner is only given to picked men of known bravery.' With no identified grave, Harold's name appears on a cemetery wall in France.

Left: A studio portrait of Emma Elizabeth Armstrong, née Abbott (1892-1970). Known as Betty, my mother had hoped to become a school teacher, but the death of her fiancé during the First World War and her eventual marriage in 1922 to a widower with four children, put paid to her own scholarly ambitions.

Below: Betty and younger sister Molly worked 'on munitions' at Kynoch's, Witton, during the Great War. This postcard – taken on 'Birmingham Win the War' day, 21 September 1918 – is one of a series illustrating Kynoch's floats, presumably designed to boost the morale of workers. Three of Betty's brothers became long-service employees of this firm, internationally renowned for its working of non-ferrous metals.

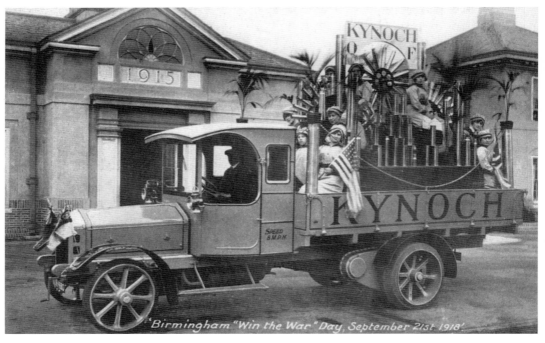

'Birmingham "Win the War" Day, September 21st 1918'.

Right: Walter Abbott (1862–1941), my maternal grandfather, is seen here with five of his seven children. Walter earned a precarious living as a jobbing gardener 'for the toffs in the posh houses up Handsworth Wood'. As a small child, I regarded him with slightly apprehensive curiosity. He could neither read nor write, his sandy moustache had been darkened as a result of drinking tea from a saucer, and he always spent Sunday afternoons in bed. This quiet, kindly man found self-expression in his beautifully tended allotment.

Below: Some of the houses on Handsworth Wood Road where my grandfather Walter Abbott may have dug and sowed. A top-hatted driver on the wrong side of the road conveys a sense of haughty disregard for lesser mortals.

HANDSWORTH WOOD ROAD

FOOD FOR THE GUNS.

Above: This postcard comes from a series of twelve cards designed to promote the War Bond Campaign. A Ministry of Munitions had been established in 1915, headed up by Lloyd George. Arguably, well-paid work on shells and bullets production did more to emancipate women than the Suffragette Movement. Over six million women worked in factories or the services during the Great War.

Left: In 1886 Selina Abbott (1863–1934), centre, exchanged domestic service for the myriad onerous services required of a working-class wife. Her extended family eventually included seven children and eighteen grandchildren. She became the central maternal figure to whom family members could turn for practical help and guidance. Although her material resources were slender, a bit of margarine, a few ounces of sugar and a 'tanner to see you home safely on the tram', and could be conjured up for the family members struggling on the dole. Fiancés, fiancées and spouses valued her advice, but 'partners' would have been matters for bridge, business or the ballroom.

two

Home
Ground

Left: Although small in stature, both Rudolph Valentino and Charlie Chaplin proved to be giant crowd pleasers during the era of silent films. During 1921 both stars enjoyed 'smash hits'. In *The Kid* Chaplin, along with Jackie Coogan playing a young orphan, made a tremendous impact on the general public, mixing comedy with pathos in masterly fashion. Often billed as 'The Screen's Greatest Lover' Valentino starred in *The Sheik*. Trading on his Latino good looks and robust love-making on the silver screen, Valentino specialised in sultry, exotic, romantic roles. His death at the age of thirty-one generated hysteria, some stage-managed, some genuine, among his legions of female fans.

Above right: A Player's Navy Cut cigarette card, showing members of the Mount Everest expedition. While the valiant attempts of 1922 and 1924 to scale Everest were unsuccessful, the fate of Mallory and Irvine has generated abiding interest. Irvine and Mallory are standing in the back row on the left.

Left: My arrival on 5 April 1923 at no. 96 Crompton Road, Handsworth, was met with appropriate interest by my immediate family. I was spared, at six months of age, the ignominy of posing in my 'birthday suit' through my mother's fear of draughts and chills. Besides, she was not averse to showing the results of her undoubted knitting skills.

CROMPTON RD. HANDSWORTH

The new grandson was duly taken to see Grandma (via Crompton Road). Two future school friends, John and Trevor Archer, lived in one of the houses on the right. In Hutton Road the large entrance to a builder's yard can be seen (centre, left), while Wilkinson is just visible to the left. The horse is probably pulling a milk float.

Westminster Rd. Perry Barr.   Nightingale.

My maternal grandparents and their two bachelor sons lived on Westminster Road, Perry Barr, near the trees in the hazy distance. Their 'parlour' was sub-let to a boot repairer. The lounge/diner was small, the scullery/kitchen minute. With no bathroom and the lavatory in the yard, their house in Westminster Road was typical of many in the city.

The wedding breakfast for cousin Madge was held at no. 96 Crompton Road. My sister Edna, seated on the left, served as a bridesmaid and brother Stan, standing on the right, as best man. The garden foliage reflects the Victorian passion for ferns while the evening's 'bit of a do' was given up to 1920s jazz, the Charleston and general high jinks.

17

In 1926 the country had blundered towards economic ruin and social collapse because of the so-called General Strike. The caption for this postcard states: 'Semi-Martial Law. Holding up Motor Cars at Perry Barr.' This may be an allusion to the emergency measures put in place at this time, including the enrolment of volunteer special constables. The Dewar's whisky advert on the railway bridge encourages thoughts of cheerier days ahead.

BREAKING THE STRIKE.

Large Numbers Of Men Return To Their Posts.

FACTORIES RESTARTING.

With no newspapers being printed, the government brought out its own broadsheet, *The British Gazette*, edited by Winston Churchill, Chancellor of the Exchequer. Under emergency powers the government divided the country into areas managed by Civil Commissioners. Extract from *The British Gazette*, Wednesday 12 May 1926:

There have been a few arrests for stone throwing at Birmingham and intimidation at Atherstone, but otherwise the situation is good.

The Birmingham Corporation have 10,000 volunteers ready at the first call to maintain all services.

The tramway men are steadily returning to work, and trams are running on several routes. The 'buses are being run by volunteers at present, but a number of 'bus drivers have offered to return. Engineers at the General Electric Company have gone back to work. One very important company re-opened its works on Monday night, and in other cases strikers are returning.

Over 2,000 special constables have been enrolled and many more are coming in.

SITUATION SHORTLY VACANT WITH GOOD PROSPECTS OF A RISE

Despite the grim, brutal realities of trench warfare, humour still prevailed on both the Western and Home Front. Bruce Bairnsfather, a young army officer with considerable experience of the war in Flanders, produced many cartoons for *The Bystander*. His stoical 'Old Bill' became a popular character.

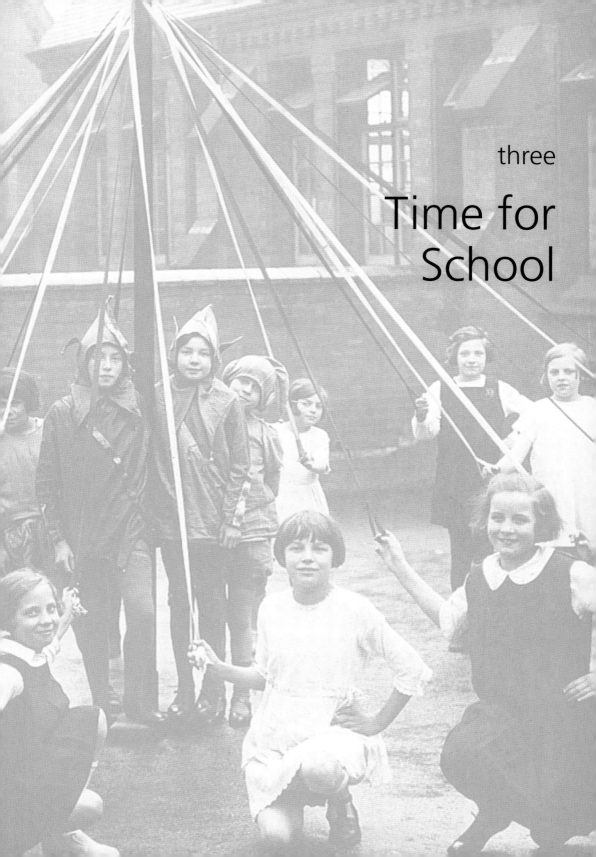

three

Time for School

Westminster Road Infants and Junior School, Birchfields, barely visible on this card, stands directly opposite the Congregational Church. The brick pillars provide the clue to the school's entrance. To the left of the two cyclists runs Putney Road, its gutters available for children's games, first with clay and later with glass marbles.

Westminster Road Infants, class 1B. Forty-two of England's finest, of whom only sixteen are boys. My best friend in 1B, Maurice Shelley, stands in the back row displaying the stoutest of braces and is the only child wearing glasses. I stand next to Maurice on his right. Many of the girls appear to have had fashion conscious mothers, evident through the bobbed hairstyles. Names that can be fitted to faces and fringes include Peggy Lawrence, Mary Clark, Audrey McKeag and Nancy Dixon. Our teacher was kind Miss Batson. The photograph was probably taken in 1929 after our first year of schooling.

This was the most thrilling part of the four sections of Crompton Road, Handsworth, for three eminently sound schoolboy reasons: it was the entrance to a cinder-surfaced path along which Maurice Shelley and I raced, scabby kneed at breakneck pace, and it housed both Mrs Brearley's parlour sweet shop where, with a small metal hammer, she broke slabs of toffeeluscious lumps, and Mr Baker's, a wonderful newsagent which sold editions of *The Wizard* every ('stick jaw') into Tuesday.

Lozells Street School, May Festival, 1928. While greatly admiring the splendidly groomed and bedecked carthorses and lavishly decorated carts that marked May Day parades, my schoolboy heart did not rejoice at maypole dancing. Dancing took place in our school hall, a special floor socket allowing the pole to be secured, ribbons of red and green, the school's colours, passed muster.

On 18 October 1929 the newly-built British airship, the *R.101*, carried out a trial flight over Birmingham. It was seen by many, myself included. While busy at games in the school playground we all suddenly fell silent, standing stock-still to gawp in wonderment at this new marvel of the skies.

Built by Boulton & Paul to establish a projected air-line between London and Australia, the largest airship in the world, the *R.101*, incorporated many new design features. On its maiden flight to India on 5 October 1930, the airship crashed at Beauvais, near Paris, and burst into flames. Only six of the fifty-four passengers survived.

In around 1930, my father was afflicted with osteomyelitis in his right knee. Through deeply invasive surgery, amputation was averted but at the cost of a permanently rigid right leg. Until the Second World War broke out in 1939 my father was never again in full-time employment. He is seen here convalescing in the Jaffray Hospital.

The Jaffray Hospital in Erdington was opened in 1885, taking its name from the founder John Jaffray (1818-1901), a Scotsman who was knighted for his philanthropic work, principally in the building and running of hospitals. This hospital remained in service until 1991.

Left: In the back garden of no. 96 Crompton Road with my father, newly returned from the Jaffray. My mother's appearance reveals the strain and nagging worries occasioned by father's illness and the family's shaky economic future – common to many families at this time. Sister Edna stands bright and perky. Note my mother's belt and braces approach to my trousers – also applied to my upbringing.

Below: A charming enactment of *Goldilocks and the Three Bears* at Eliot Street Infants School in the days of gas lighting. Presumably the girl sitting at the front with a posy on her lap is Goldilocks. The porridge bowls seem appropriately scaled.

Edna marries Sam Eldridge in 1932. The male Eldridges are stylishly dressed, note the white bow ties and Sam's fashionable spats, but Father and my brother Jack, both standing to the couple's left simply wear their Sunday best. My mother still looks ill compared to the bonny bridesmaids, Grace and Gladys.

Heathfield Road, Handsworth. Among the group of shops on the right-hand side stood a hardware shop managed by Sam Eldridge. Nearby, a virtual Aladdin's cave of a newsagents-cum-toy shop displayed its boy-tantalising wares. By rigorous self-denial, I amassed in this shop's Christmas Club fund the princely sum of fourteen shillings and sixpence. A renowned Bowman stationary steam engine became mine!

B.C.S. Grocery Display at the B.C.S. Jubilee Exhibition,1931. More than a dozen different postcards commemorated aspects of the Golden Jubilee Exhibition of the Birmingham Co-operative Society held in Bingley Hall in 1931. Our family used two of the 105 grocery branches mentioned on the card, one in Crompton Road and the other, much larger, in Birchfield Road, Perry Barr, which adjoined a Co-op bakers, butchers and greengrocers.

Another postcard advertising the B.C.S. Dairy Display in the B.C.S. Jubilee Exhibition of 1931. Our milk and bread were efficiently delivered to the door by Co-op rounds-men. In 1932, for every pound spent, 1s and 2d (nearly 6 per cent) would be paid into customer's dividend accounts; divvy proved a godsend to many a working-class mother when buying children's clothing and footwear.

This photograph of a wedding car in Lincoln Street evokes memories of my own errand boy experiences. Duties ranged from the safe transport of fragile gas mantles and mouth-watering basinfuls of faggots and peas, to the delivery of wire-bound bundles of firewood, brown paper bags of bird seed, assorted groceries and the right change from a ten bob note.

City of Birmingham Education Committee.

Admission Examination to Secondary Schools.

WEDNESDAY, 14TH MARCH, 1934.   9.30—10.15.

ARITHMETIC I.

Do as many as you can of the following sums.
Show all your working.
Cross out boldly any work you do not wish the Examiner
  to read.
In No. 1 you need not copy the sum.   You may write the
  answer only on your paper.

1.
$$
\begin{array}{rrr}
£ & s. & d. \\
1,753 & 9 & 4 \\
428 & 14 & 5\frac{1}{2} \\
4,517 & 8 & 7 \\
87,265 & 12 & 10\frac{3}{4}
\end{array}
$$
£93965 - 5 - 3½

2. 307,105—8,217.   298,888
3. 3,519 × 73.   256,887
4. 71,438 ÷ 29.   2463¾
5. Find $\frac{1}{7}$ of £90 13s. 4d.   £64 - 0 - 0
6. $\dfrac{2 \cdot 7 \times 0 \cdot 084 \times 5 \cdot 28}{0 \cdot 028 \times 10 \cdot 8 \times 3}$ 1·32

7. Simplify :—
   (a) $\dfrac{£5 \; 8s. \; 4d.}{£5 \; 16s. \; 8d.}$ $\frac{13}{14}$ (b) 2·3 × 1·03   2·369
   (c) $\dfrac{1 \text{ ton } 1 \text{ cwt.}}{3 \text{ tons}}$ $\frac{7}{20}$ (d) 19·2 ÷ 0·4   48

8. (a) $11\frac{5}{8}$ yards — $8\frac{1}{2}$ yards + $\frac{3}{4}$ yard. Write your answer
       in yards, feet and inches.   3½
   (b) $\frac{3}{4}$ of $6\frac{1}{2}$ gallons. Write your answer in gallons, quarts,
       pints.
   (c) $3\frac{1}{4}$ tons ÷ 4. Write your answer in cwts. and lbs.
9. What percentage is 1 chain of half a mile?   2½%.

Left: Part of the '11 plus' of its day, 'pure'
and 'applied' arithmetic in this case.
Examination success meant possible entry to
a grammar school.

Below: Westminster Road Junior Cricket
Team, 1934. From the left to right, back
row: Norman Ludlow, Jackie Hubbard,
Ronnie Inshaw, Gordon Rixom, ?, Trevor
Archer, Ronnie Jordan, Stanley Hopcroft.
Middle row: ? Willetts, Mr Clayton (the
newly-appointed headmaster), Alan Griffiths,
Mr Archer, (the new sports master), ? Pine.
Front row: Harry Dawson, ? Walsh, Eric
Armstrong.

WESTMINSTER Rd JUNIOR CRICKET TEAM 1934.

four

1934-1937

An early postcard of Victoria Park, Handsworth. My walk to and from Handsworth Grammar School included a complete crossing of Victoria Park, following the railings in the foreground, then turning right onto a path flanked by a rhododendron jungle – a quiet stretch which allowed a certain teenage boy to reflect darkly on the injustices of homework.

The three pedestrians on the right-hand side of this card are walking towards the park gate on Grove Lane, Handsworth. The 26 tram is travelling towards the public baths before reaching its terminus in Oxhill Road.

A useful, if arguably overly-ornate, drinking fountain in Handsworth Park. Part of the tower of St Mary's Church can be seen in the distance.

This fountain-cum-paddling pool in Handsworth Park provides smashing, splashing fun for at least two dozen children on this hot summer day. The adult on the far right is looking across the boating pool.

Grove Hall in Grove Lane, a private house bought by Handsworth Urban District Council in 1887 to serve as a park facility. A 'Cadbury's Chocolate' advert can be seen in the lower right window. Crown, not rink, bowling was played on this green and many others in Birmingham. The card was posted in 1932.

When Handsworth formed part of Staffordshire, the above bridge at Perry Barr was kept repaired by a trust. The trust's objectives were later converted to educational purposes leading to the school's founding in 1862 hence the representation of the zigzag bridge in the school's badge, surmounted by the Staffordshire knot.

Handsworth Park afforded fine opportunities for the younger generation to let off steam. 'Nodding off' would come later. The building is the boathouse, a ridged slipway can be seen to its left.

Above: Handsworth Grammar School for Boys, where those who strove to push back the frontiers of ignorance toiled.

Right: A rather austere welcome perhaps, but the headmaster seems well aware that some of the 1934 intake to Handsworth Grammar School will come from relatively poor families with no previous experience of what a grammar school education entails.

HANDSWORTH GRAMMAR SCHOOL,

Grove Lane,

Birmingham, 21.

Dear Parents,

    School opens at 9 o'clock on September 11th when I shall be glad to see your son.

    I enclose a statement of Rules and Suggestions. It has been prepared in order to give your boy every advantage here, and it is particularly desired that you shall feel there is every wish to save you expense. The equipment should be obtained as required, and not all at once. School caps (which bear the 'Bridge' on the front) may be obtained early in September from local outfitters.

    There is also attached a Book List which I ask you to sign and return to me after crossing out the books already obtained. Approved Second Hand Books may be purchased at the School at 10.30 a.m. on Saturday, July 21st. The completed Book List should be returned to me by Monday 23rd of July, failing which I shall assume you yourself will arrange for the boy to have the books for use on the first day of term.

    I ask you to encourage the boy to prepare his work at home carefully and to interest himself fully in School work and play. Apathy and indolence must fail, but interest and steady endeavour are equally sure of obtaining success.

    I sincerely hope your son will enjoy a very healthy and happy life with us.

                Yours sincerely,

(Signed)   J. J. Walton, M.A., B.Sc..

                Head Master.

Head Master.
J. J. WALTON, M.A. B.Sc.

Second Master.
T. H. THOMAS, B.A.

Assistant Masters.

G. M. Hilbourne, B. Sc.	E. Knight, B.A.
H. A. Allison, B.A.	F. E. Western, B. Sc.
E. S. Guise, B. A.	C. J. Cox, B. A.
K. L. Kenrick, M.A.	K. A. Sprayson, B.Sc.
Miss Dingley.	L. L. Lindley, B.A.
A. Lindon, B.A.	G. H. Malkee, M.A.
Miss Keeling, B.A.	E. P. Icke, B.Sc.
C. A. Brooke, B.A.	A. P. Lawrence, B.Sc.
A. R. W. Hutchinson,M.Sc.	H. W. Stubbington,
F. G. Gaydoul, B.A.	F.R.C.O.
B. W. Llewellyn.	A. N. Court, B.A.
S. R. Sheppard, B.A.	L. E. Innes, D.P.E.
	H. Bligh, D.L.C.

Secretary.
Miss I. Brock, B.A.

Head Prefect.
G. Gibson.

Prefects.

R. J. Worrall.	D. E. Yeomans.
H. R. Jones.	N. P. Jackson.
D. W. Price.	D. J. Rigby.
R. L. Whitmore.	P. R. Griffith.
S. G. Hughes.	D. Austin.
L. Wood.	

Left: An unofficial list of staff at the school in 1940. In random order, they inlcude Hulu, Sally, Peck. Holy Joe, Sammy, Baggy, Gogs, Poona, Wesser, Scratch, Stubby.

Below: Homeward bound, satchel bulging with homework, an alternative route through Handsworth Park could be taken across the footbridge over the railway, to encounter a scene similar to the above. Handsworth Wood station (1896-1941) was located in Hamstead Road. Alternatively, a saunter round the boating pool could be pleasant.

Above: An early view of St Mary's Church. St Mary's, dating back to the twelfth century, is the parish church of Handsworth in Hamstead Road, and last resting place of Boulton, Watt and Murdock. On a hot day I would call at the corner sweet shop opposite the church for a glass of pop.

Below: Given the rapid growth of motor traffic during the 'thirties, restrictions were placed on speeding in built-up areas, a speed limit of 30mph being imposed in 1935. Police cars fitted with gongs were expected to stop offenders. Even one of the tobacco firm giants, Wills, was moved to issue a series of fifty traffic Safety cards in 1934.

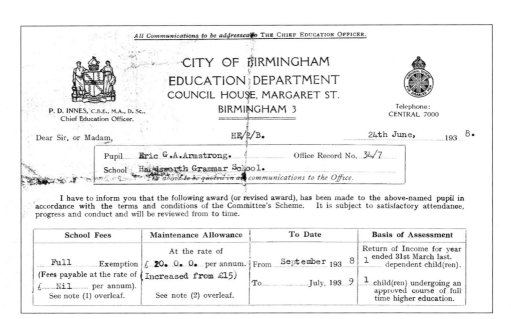

CITY OF BIRMINGHAM
EDUCATION DEPARTMENT
COUNCIL HOUSE, MARGARET ST.
BIRMINGHAM 3

P. D. INNES, C.B.E., M.A., D.Sc.,
Chief Education Officer.

Telephone:
CENTRAL 7000

Dear Sir, or Madam,　　　　　HE/2/B.　　　　24th June, 193 8.

Pupil　Eric G.A.Armstrong.　　　　Office Record No. 34/7

School　Handsworth Grammar School.

The above to be quoted in all communications to the Office.

I have to inform you that the following award (or revised award), has been made to the above-named pupil in accordance with the terms and conditions of the Committee's Scheme. It is subject to satisfactory attendance, progress and conduct and will be reviewed from to time.

School Fees	Maintenance Allowance	To Date	Basis of Assessment
Full Exemption (Fees payable at the rate of £ Nil per annum). See note (1) overleaf.	At the rate of £ 20. 0. 0. per annum. (Increased from £15) See note (2) overleaf.	From September 193 8 To July, 193 9	Return of Income for year ended 31st March last. 1 dependent child(ren). 1 child(ren) undergoing an approved course of full-time higher education.

In September 1935 I moved class from 1c to Remove C, one of the two fast-track forms. Being from an 'economically disadvantaged' family, I received first a book allowance, subsequently replaced by a maintenance allowance. The fifteen books bought for me in September 1935 by the City of Birmingham Education Committee cost a princely total of £1 9s 10d. Surprisingly one of the books remains a sturdy evergreen, the incomparable 'Pickwick Papers'.

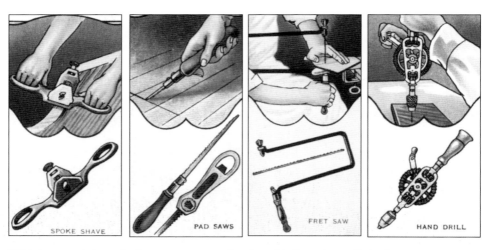

With its crowded curriculum, a grammar school could allocate very little time to non-academic subjects. Yet woodwork was a highly popular lesson at Handsworth Grammar School due largely to the personality and ability of the teacher, Mr A.C. Tytherleigh. After his premature death, a very warm tribute to this man appeared in *The Bridge*, the school magazine, Midsummer Term 1937. These cigarette cards are from a series by Carreras Ltd entitled 'Tools and How to Use Them'.

Nineteen of the twenty-four young bridge builders, and two of the teachers, can be named in this class picture. They are, in no particular order: Frank Collins, Fred Boon, Leslie Gloster, Reg Burkenshaw, Fred Barnes, Arthur Cox, Mr Williams, George Dawson, Arthur Quance, William Goldby, William Poole, Tom Johnson, Arthur Robinson, Ronald Phillips, Guy Box, Arthur Mason, Victor Sewell, Horace Walford, George Gough, Leslie Pilnick, Mr Meggett. From the clothing worn, this is almost certainly a pre-First World War photograph, thought to have been taken at Wattville Road School, Handsworth. The model may have been based on the Clifton Suspension Bridge, Bristol.

HMS *Birmingham* Athough as far from the coast as it is possible for an English town or city to be, Birmingham took a close interest in its nameskae warship.

My first visit to the seaside came in 1937. Mother's bachelor brothers Arthur and George took me on holiday to Babbacombe, Devon. For most of the time, I was happily left to my own devices. Uncle George is seated on a bollard.

A Gallery of Sporting Fame – one schoolboy's choice. Clockwise, from top left: 'April the Fifth' – winner of the Derby in 1932, jockey F. Lane, starting price 100–6. My Mum won a few bob on this horse, my birthday falling on 5 April; My role model Jack Lovelock from New Zealand, he won the 1,500m at the 1936 Olympic games in Berlin at a record time of 3 minutes 47.8 seconds; Born in Dudley in 1909, Dot Round was the Wimbledon winner of the Women's Singles in 1934; G.V. Barna, world champion table tennis player from Hungary; To quote Wisden: 'Suffering from tonsillitis, Paynter left a hospital bed to play an historic four-hour innings of 83. Later he struck the six which won the match and regained the Ashes' in Brisbane, 1933.

five

1938

The Melody Maker.

The harmonica was popular with 1930s boys, being light, small and fitting easily into trouser or jacket pockets. Larry Adler became a virtuoso of the instrument but I also admired, from broadcasts and records, the happy-go-lucky, knockabout style of Borrah Minevitch and his Harmonica Rascals.

DUDLEY
BUXTON

" Got any cigarette pictures, guvnor? "

This postcard by noted artist Dudley Buxton is typical of many illustrating the zeal but bad timing of cigarette card collectors. Having various male smokers in the family, I had little need to stoop to pestiferous urchin tactics to add to my collection.

This cover, July 1937, was not a bad attempt at futurology! This *Flying Aces* magazine bought from Woolworths contains an article on the 'apron or wire net' as a means of defence.

On Saturday evenings my best friend Alan and I would saunter up and down Lozells Road seeking young ladies to chat-up – although an early card, little had changed. Berners Street is on the right, and Hartington Road on the left.

DOUGH MAKING ROOM AT GEORGE BAINES' MODEL BAKERY.

If the timing of a walk to the Lozells was right, we would linger in Finch Road, noses in the air, bliss on our faces, like Bisto kids, as we inhaled the baking fragrances emanating from 'Baines' Model Bakery'. This is one of a series of promotional cards.

Sundays meant a lie-in before a late breakfast, while afternoons were spent in Sunday school at Westminster Road Congregational Church. 'High tea' at 'Grans' usually consisted of tinned salmon or sardines, with pineapple chunks to follow. When my grandmother died in 1934, mother exchanged her job as charwoman in a dairy on the Lichfield Road for housekeeper to her father, two brothers and occasional lodger. So, wind up the portable gramophone, put on a 78 and snigger to the reedy, crackling words of 'Horsey! Keep your tail up, Keep the Sun out of my Eyes' – a rather bizarre request!

My father exchanged occasional drinks at The Stork, on the corner of Heathfield and Finch Roads, for a jug of ale from the off-licence across the road from our new home. 'Adam's Ale' (Welsh tap water) made good any liquid deficiency.

Stalwarts of class 5C in Handsworth Park during a dinner break, from left to right: John Archer, Alsop, Eric Armstrong, 'Wiffy' Pearce. Now in my fourth year at school, I was better able to understand, and partly agree with, what the energetic and dedicated headmaster, the Reverend J.J. Walton, was trying to achieve, i.e. marked improvements to academic, social, sporting and cultural standards. The headmaster was also the driving force for the school's series of annual Gilbert and Sullivan presentations. It was widely held that in the *Mikado* he made a very natural Pooh-Bah.

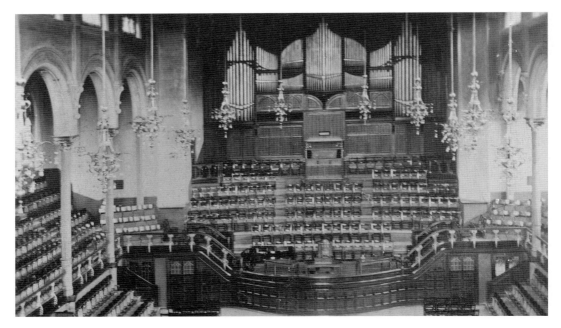

Interior of the Central Hall, an impressive redbrick structure in Corporation Street housed the 'HQ' of the Methodist Church in Birmingham. In November 1938 school Speech Day was also held in the Hall.

Located at Castle Bromwich, the British Industries Fair, held from 1920 onwards, provided an annual showcase to promote British trade. The swag, sample bits of glass wool, plywood etc, collected by Alan and myself would now be known as freebies.

Elijah was presented by the Handsworth Grammar School choir at St Martin's Church, Bull Ring.

Tuesday 3 May: *Date for tomorrow night by bandstand. With Alan and myself.* Next evening, *Muriel very fast. Date for Friday same place* … another complete frost for neither of the two girls appeared. Uneducated in music and dance, untutored in social skills, at least of the flirting kind, the girlfriend outlook seemed bleak. In this context, 'fast' signified racy to the point of risqué.

A 1930s council estate expands. This northern bus terminus (29 and 29a services) on Kingstanding Road gave access to a variety of pleasures, including the mock baronial Kingstanding public house, a walk up Rough Road to Sutton Park, and an Odeon cinema.

Banners Gate, Sutton Park.

Whatever his motives, in bequeathing land in 1528 that would later become the 2,400 acres of Sutton Park, Henry VIII did a great service to Birmingham people, especially during the inter-war years when the park offered a fine place for a 'grand day out'. Heath land, woodlands and seven pools remained much as nature intended.

Above: On 11 July 1938 Birmingham began a week-long pageant to celebrate its centenary as a city. The historic Aston Hall in Aston Park provided the main stage for the re-enactment of relevant historical events such as the siege of Aston Hall during the English Civil War and the visit to Aston Park by Queen Victoria in 1858.

Right: This statue formed part of one of the two floral fountains erected at each end of Broad Street. Apparently it symbolised a young 'smith bestriding the city, represented by the model of the Council House. Whatever local people made of this artwork, it was certainly a touch avant garde for its day! But then, the city's motto is 'Forward'!

Summer holidays, ample time to spare but no Devonshire cream tea this year. Netherton and Windmill End housed twelve of my Black Country cousins.

A country of hard workers on canals, in pits, factories and ironworks. The card shows chain testing at Lloyds Proving House in Netherton, *c.* 1929. At one time, Hingley & Sons of Netherton was the largest cable and anchor manufacturer in the world. The *Titanic's* anchors were made by this firm.

The entrance to Perry Park, Perry Barr. In terms of prestige, homely Perry Park used to lag behind Handsworth and Canon Hill Parks until it became home to the Alexander Sports Stadium of international status.

Monday 12 September: *Went to Perry Park this afternoon. Got to know two very nice girls; Amy, Margaret … Alan and I took them home after Guides.*

These cigarette cards come from a number of tobacco companies, namely Copes, Anstie's and Player's.

Friday 16 September: *Great life in VI.* Eighteen free periods. More time for swimming perhaps.
This early postcard shows schoolboys outside Gove Lane, Handsworth, public baths.

Sunday 18 September: *Went to Grove Lane baths in the morning.*
Built in 1907 the Grove Lane baths in Handsworth provided separate entrances for men and
women until mixed bathing became increasingly popular. The photograph appears to show a gala
event, probably pre-First World War, given the style of costumes and suits. The ladies are thought
to be members of the Handsworth Swimming Club.

During my sixth-form years at school I spent many enjoyable Saturday evenings at the Villa Cross Picture House in Handsworth. The card shows the cinema's foyer as it was in May 1916, although it was much the same in 1938.

Wednesday 28 September: *Hitler, Musso, Daladier* (the French Premier) *and Chamberlain at Munich. Evacuation scheme at school! But I'm not going!*
Thursday 29 September. *Went round to schools this morning giving out gasmasks. Six of us gave out nearly 4,000. Hard work.*

Sunday 20 November: *Went to Carr's Lane in afternoon. Congregational Rally.*
My church-going commitments had grown as a result of my ulterior-motivated secular interests.
After attending evening service at Westminster Road Church I would literally dash to meet Amy
and Margaret at St Mary's Church.

Margaret attended Rose Hill Road School in Handsworth; a prestigious school for girls which
celebrated its centenary in 1983.

six

1939

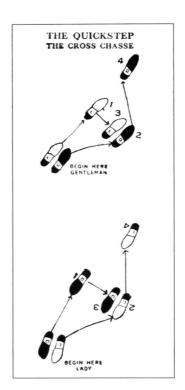

Above: Wednesday 11 January: *Copied instructions for dancing from a book this morning and practised steps – in the form room, chairs and desks pushed to one side, steps chalked on the floor.*

Competency at ballroom dancing often seemed the way to a girl's embrace!

Left: Saturday 4 February: *Listened to Henry Hall.*

In 1932 Henry Hall (1898-1989) followed Jack Payne as head of the BBC Dance Orchestra and soon became immensely popular, particularly with his version of *The Teddy Bear's Picnic*. Henry's radio programmes 'signed on' with *It's Just the Time for Dancing* and 'signed off' with the breezy *Here's to the Next Time*.

Jack Payne and his band. Jack Payne (1899-1969) was once a pupil at Rookery Road Council School, Handsworth, before attending Handsworth Grammar School where he became a prominent member of the school's Officer Training Corps. After joining the Royal Flying Corps during the Great War he won his wings, becoming a first lieutenant at the age of eighteen. *Say it with Music* was his well known signature tune.

Monday 6 March: Margaret and I *have moved our 'au revoir' spot further along West Avenue in Cherry Orchard* – an area of quite new, private houses, each, undoubtedly, with a bathroom.

Monday 21 March: *Saw part of a balloon barrage this dinner-time. Think it is in Aston Park.*
Soon there would be many more in position. The balloon barrage formed one of the important lines of defence by defeating attempts on the part of the enemy to fly over and bomb British territory.

High Bridges, Great Barr.

The annual school cross–country race included running across this high bridge in Newton Road, Great Barr. In 1939 I managed to struggle in fourth.

A view up Newton Road, Great Barr, taken from Queslett Road. Walsall Road runs left towards Birmingham, while Birmingham Road, on the right, leads towards Walsall. The Scott Arms, a Mitchells and Butler public house, stands on the corner.

The Guild was, in effect, a first rate youth club which I regularly attended with Alan – and later on with Margaret who, too often for male pride, beat me at table tennis. Meetings were held weekly – the programme included speakers, socials, debates and 'spiffing dances'.

𝕱riends' 𝕳all,

Farm Street.

Young People's Guild.

𝕾eason 1938=39.

Opening September 8th, 1938

at 7-30 p.m.

YOUNG PEOPLE CORDIALLY WELCOMED.

The Colliery, Hamstead.

Above: Thursday 27 April: *Saw John* [Archer]. *Had a good ramble by Hamstead. Watched the workings of the colliers.*

At the time, Hamstead was very much a mining village. Although adjoining the northern edge of Handsworth, the miners' cottages did not really seem part of Birmingham.

Left: The Hamstead pit disaster of 4 March 1908 had not faded from local memory. An underground fire trapped a large number of miners. Some men did escape including Mr F. Jones, seen here, the last man to escape, but eventually twenty-five bodies were recovered. Seventy-six pit ponies also died.

Left: This photograph shows me with my Uncle George, cycle clips in place, in my grandmother's backgarden. By winning the long jump, quarter mile and one mile, I became Senior Athletic Champion at school. Uncle George had won cups himself for bowls and snooker at Lea Hall, the local Working Men's Club in Wood Lane. Behind can be seen the radio aerial pole and a shed doubling as an aviary (well stocked with bird seed by a certain errand boy!)

Below: On 14 June the Bishop of Birmingham opened a newly-built wing at Handsworth Grammar School. This contained physics and chemistry labs and 'a splendid, lavishly equipped gymnasium' where, for some curious reason, I enjoyed climbing a rope hanging from the ceiling, feet rather than head first.

Perry Barr, a busy shopping centre, witnessed the following unusual agreement, as recorded in my diary:

Sunday 2 July: *Amusing argument with Eddie and Evan … Laid £5 bet that Eddie will be married before he is thirty-two. He firmly avows that he will not.*

I think I won but have no recollection of a fiver coming my way.

BIRMINGHAM, AIRPORT.

Above: Saturday 8 July. *Terrific downpour...saw Margaret...stood in rain from half past 12 to half past 5...excellent ariel display...Spitfires, Hurricanes, Blenheims, Skuas...Duchess of Kent, Chamberlain and Crump...Quagmire. Trousers practically ruined.*

The rain-sodden opening of Birmingham Airport, Elmdon.

Left: Saturday 15 July: *Eddie and I went to ARP Rally in Handsworth Park... Blazing house put out... Anti-Aircraft guns in action ... Hitler will run up against a packet if he takes us on.*

My approach was more patriotic than realistic. War was now more a probability than possibility.

A tranquil scene featuring the now listed Calthorpe Cottages on Wood Lane, Handsworth.

Above: At Abergele in 1939, where I took my summer holiday with the school camp. After a mixed bag of weather and experiences my spirits rose. When packing the lorry with sodden tents before heading for Brum, a letter arrived from Margaret. She wrote 'au revoir'. Hopeful after a quarrel!

Right: On 5 August I listed in my diary half a dozen pals who were all away somewhere on holiday or, like Doug Sandin, in gainful employment. Generous Uncle George had lent me his bike, so I set about exploring an area north of Birmingham. Lichfield Cathedral impressed me greatly.

Wednesday 30 August: *Staggered reluctantly to school this morning* – three weeks early – for evacuation briefing. *Had to take message to Miss Brew's study at Rose Hill Road School. Girls in hall. Sounded like a cage of parrots.*

On the morning of Friday 1 September 1939, 351 boys accompanied by twenty-six masters and helpers left New Street Station for Stroud. I remained at home for two reasons: evacuation was not compulsory and my parents disagreed about whether I should continue at school or go to work.

Right: Wednesday 23 August: *Listened to 'Radiolympia'. News very grave. Russo German pact in full form. All householders told to get material to darken their windows.*

At this time the Russian–German Non-Aggression pact was fully operational, yet we still found things to amuse us, particularly the radio.

Far right: Despite events abroad, some of the normal features of peacetime life were restored. Cinemas re-opened after being temporarily closed for fear of air raids, and football games resumed.

Saturday 23 Sept. *Westcott a real live wire leader for the Wolves. Banged in three peach goals…against the 'Baggies'* West Bromwich Albion. I'd walked to the Hawthorns for this derby match.

The tug-of-war between my parents about my future was decided by the City Education Committee, in my mother's favour. So, greatly rejoicing, I travelled to Stroud in Gloucestershire by coach on 29 October to join Herbert Sharpley (Syd) in a very snug billet. Our formal schooling was carried out at the Marling School for boys, above.

Our splendid if elderly 'foster parents' were Mr and Mrs Wheatley, caretakers for a town centre school who also lived on the premises. On the evening of my arrival, we played chess and crib. Points to note – chess board improvised from old pastry board, squares marked out with chalk, incipient and arguably insipid kiss curl. (Photograph courtesy of Syd)

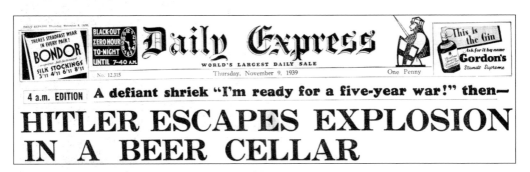

On Thursday 9 November 1939 an attempt on Hitler's life is reported in *The Daily Express* as follows:

Twenty-seven minutes after Hitler ended a hysterical speech in the Buergerbrau beer cellar at Munich last night – a speech in which he cried that he was ready for a five-years war with Britain – the building was shaken by an explosion which killed six members of the 'Old Guard' of the Nazi party, and injured sixty other people.

Hitler had already left and was not hurt. He left earlier than he originally intended as he was summoned back to Berlin by important state business.

Note the blackout times printed above the headline: 'Black-out zero hour to-night until 7.40 a.m.'

By this time, *Bandwagon*, introduced in 1938, had become an immensely popular comic radio show. Arthur Askey and Richard Murdoch, who supposedly lived in the flat over the BBC building, involved dippy characters such as Mrs Bagwash and her daughter Nausea. 'Ay thank yew! Big Hearted Arthur they call me…'

Monday 27 November: *Went to the Gaumont with Mrs W. and S. Great dancing by Ginger Rogers and Fred Astaire.*
The film we all greatly enjoyed was *The Story of Vernon and Irene Castle* based on the life of the most famous dance pairing before the Great War.

Thursday 21 December. Home Coming. *Very happy to see Mom and Dad again*. The train home arrived where it had left – New Street Station, Birmingham.

Friday 22 December. *Give me the wide open spaces* of the English Countryside. HMG (his Majesty's Government) duly obliged, later, via the army!

seven

1940

Villa Cross, Handsworth.

Above: Monday 1 January: *Saw Margaret (home from Worcester) she looked grand. Went to the Villa Cross picture house, but she wouldn't let me hold her hand. OK afterwards though for she allowed me to kiss her goodbye.*

Left: Friday 12 January: *Letter from Dad advising me not to get a copy of 'War Illustrated'. Very sharp frost again and it is very cold. Stoked the school fires.*

We were helping Mrs Wheatley to keep the school boilers going. Eventually we took on the work under her supervision.

Tuesday 23 January: He who dares – can often come a cropper!
But my luck, like the ice, held. Three of us cycled to the Severn which, as the above photograph shows, had frozen over. Prolonged frost, snow and icy cold made 1940 one of the harshest winters of the twentieth century. That evening I saw Beau Geste twice at the Ritz.

Wednesday 14 February: *Acted as a patient for Frank. Bandaged me up all over the place.*
Frank Wheatley later became a factory manager, but had yet to take his first aid test.

Monday 19 February: *Walked through Handsworth Park. Boat house roof down. Pond still frozen.*
Mr Wheatley's continuing illness necessitated our moving to another billet. At half-term I went home
and found Birmingham slowly recovering from the severe pasting dealt by the hostile Arctic weather.

Life at Stafford House, the new billet, was not congenial to either the hosts, the Robertsons,
or their two evacuees – yet heated house bricks, wrapped in flannel, for our chilly beds was
a thoughtful touch by Mrs Robertson. For evening entertainment I continued my diary
records, and enjoyed the ongoing adventures of Young Bill.

Sunday 25 February: *Severn Stoke – pretty little place. Margaret late as usual but she looked grand.*
At this time Margaret was attending a convent school in Worcester.

HGS photograph, 1940. Pupils include: Dann, Barrett, Thompson, Sharpley, Pigott, Davies, Millichip, Heath, Madeley, Sanders, Deeley, Forster, Saunders, Davenport, Burnell, Hayward, Burton, Bendall, Potter, Anderson, Armstrong, Rees, McKenzie, Kent, Escott, Bendall, Blakemore, Saint, Startin, Deakin Seers, Grainger, Peakin, Viggers, Heath, Griffiths, Hood, Stroud, Walters, Swinfern, Quance. The adults are Mrs Pritchard (housekeeper), Mrs Lindon and Mr Lindon. All are evacuee 'tenants' of 'Northfield', Folly Lane.

Above: Northfield, in Folly Lane, a large private house, which eventually became 'home' for about fifty boys of varying ages. The advance party numbered fourteen, including Syd, Coe, Shaw, Heath, Millichip and Madeley. On Friday 8 March I wrote in my diary: *Not too bad a lot … the house has two greenhouses, conservatory, common-room, tennis court.*

Left: The noisy and boisterous inmates were under the benign supervision of Mr Baggy Lindon, senior French master, and his wife. Senior boys were put in charge of 'dormitories'.

Above: Wednesday 20 March (Easter break): *What a difference between the clean open countryside of Stroud with its frolicking lambs and shooting buds and the filth and grime of Birmingham... a pall of gloom like that of smoke over the city settled over our compartment of our train as we came back into Birmingham.*

Even so, I looked forward to the three weeks at home.

Right: Because there had been no air raids of consequence for a while, many boys remained at home in Birmingham after the Easter break instead of returning to school, prompting the following letter from the headmaster.

```
                          Handsworth Grammar School,

                          At   Marling School,

                               Stroud.

                          22nd April, 1940.

My dear Parents,

               I am sure you will be happy to know that the
School has settled down quite happily for the Summer term.
There have been many rumours as to what is to happen in the
future, both at Stroud and in Birmingham.  At the moment,
there is absolutely nothing official to my knowledge regard-
ing any change in the evacuation policy.  You may rely upon
me to let you know immediately I am so advised.

               From the many letters and talks I have had
with parents I know you appreciate all the difficulties of
administration, and would not wish to add to our problems.
I ask you, therefore, not to appeal to me for any changes
during the term.  Our work will be better done and our minds
set free by knowing exactly where we stand, and re-ensuring a
stabilized position for the summer term.  Towards the end
of the term I shall be writing you again, and asking your
wishes with regard to place of education.  You will then be
quite free to choose Stroud or Birmingham.  During the term,
however, I cannot make any changes.  It may well be that
the next few weeks will solve our problems for us, but I shall
feel bound to stand by the Government policy, whatever is
decided.  I deeply appreciate all you have done in establishing
a good solid front, in accordance with the Government wishes.
The unity of the School, procured by voluntary effort, is a
matter for commendation.  It expresses the right attitude and
is an answer in a small way to a thoroughly debased enemy.

               I shall be glad if you will send along tuition
and sports fees by Monday next, the 29th April, where this has
not already been done.

               I should like to have seen you at the School
Athletic Sports on Thursday next, but I feel sure the boys
will enjoy the contest.

               With every good wish to each one of you and
your families.
```

Left: I returned to school in Stroud after the Easter holiday and, although I trained hard, I knew I should be up against it in the school sports. Last year's Intermediate Champion, John Trevor, a fine runner, was now a senior; his legs longer than ever. In our three shared events he beat me fair and square into second place.

Below: Wednesday 8 May. *Dennis bought my bus ticket – half-price at 4/6. Shall have to have a good shave on Friday in order to diddle the bus company.* My school chum Dennis was twelve or thirteen years of age at this time, so he didn't have to pay the full bus fare. Clearly, on one particular day I was slightly over zealous with a razor, note the chin plaster. From left to right: 'Perge' Pigott, R.A.S. Rees, Syd Sharpley, Eric Armstrong.

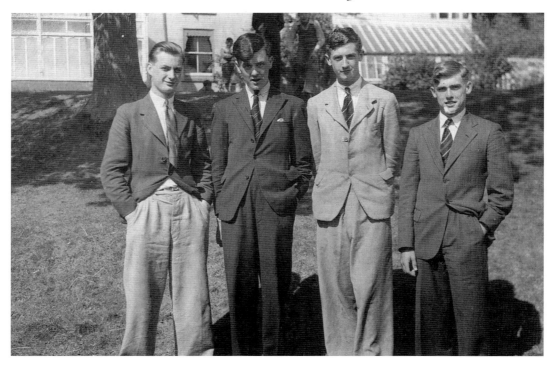

EVENING STANDARD, May 10, 1940

LATE SPECIAL

This is the Gin Gordon's Stands Supreme

Amusements 10
Radio 10

BLACK-OUT 9.5 pm, 4.47 am.
MOON Rose 7.37 am; Sets 11.24 pm.

No. 36,093   LONDON, FRIDAY, MAY 10, 1940   ONE PENNY

Evening Standard

NAZIS INVADE HOLLAND, BELGIUM, LUXEMBURG: MANY AIRPORTS BOMBED
Allies Answer Call for Aid: R.A.F. Planes are in Action

In dramatic fashion the Phoney War suddenly exploded into smithereens. A copy of the London *Evening Standard* from 10 May 1940 stated that: 'Hitler has invaded Holland, Belgium and Luxemburg. His parachute troops are landing at scores of points and many airports are being bombed.'

Now in my last term at school, revision swotting began in earnest. Northfield domestic chores, on a rough and ready roster system, were almost relentless – washing up and drying up, barrowing fuel, pruning roses, cutting the grass of the tennis court. A break was needed. Photographed by Syd Snapper are, from left to right: Ras, Pergot and Eric playing cards by Cranham Woods on Sunday 19 May.

Daily Express

No. 12,487   Friday, May 31, 1940   One Penny

Through an inferno of bombs and shells the B.E.F. is crossing the Channel from Dunkirk—in history's strangest armada

TENS OF THOUSANDS SAFELY HOME ALREADY

Many more coming by day and night

SHIPS OF ALL SIZES DARE THE GERMAN GUNS

UNDER THE GUNS OF THE BRITISH FLEET, UNDER THE WINGS OF THE ROYAL AIR FORCE, A LARGE PROPORTION OF THE B.E.F. WHO FOR THREE DAYS HAD BEEN FIGHTING THEIR WAY BACK TO THE FLANDERS COAST, HAVE NOW BEEN BROUGHT SAFELY TO ENGLAND FROM DUNKIRK.

How the Allies fought back to Dunkirk, aided by warships and planes. British troops held the left flank, French troops the right flank. Last rear-guard action (see inset) fought by French under General Prioux on the hills between Cassel and Ypres.

The near miraculous evacuation from Dunkirk, as reported in the *Daily Express* on Friday 31 May 1940.

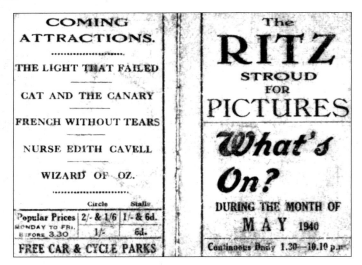

Even though the world had become a dangerous and scary place, temporary escapism remained ready to hand in the form of the Ritz cinema in Stroud. This programme details films showing during the month of May 1940. Other films shown this month included *The Star Maker* starring Bing Crosby and Ned Sparks, and *The Real Glory* starring Gary Cooper and David Niven.

Opposite: Friday 14 June: A testing day. *Paris has fallen. Went up to the University in Edmund Street with John and Syd for oral examination in French. Seems a little ironic.* Bien sûr! Quel dommage.

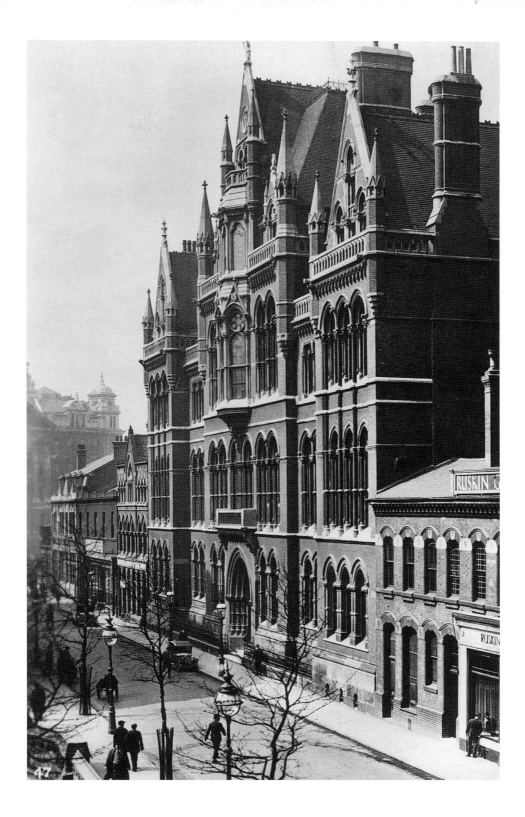

47

I left school in the summer of 1940 after finishing my exams, and returned home to Birmingham. *Friday 26 July: Arrived at Gloucester where Dennis and I caught a local train to Worcester. Rotten having to say goodbye to one's pals … leant out of the carriage window to say goodbye to Margaret – whistle went and our lips met as of mutual accord. She returned my blown kiss, as the train steamed out of the station.*

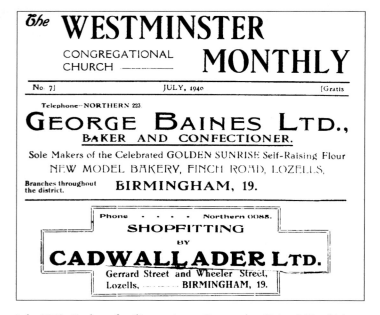

July 1940. Back to familiar territory. Remember Baines? Dunkirk was still a fresh and vivid memory for many, as evidenced by personal experience accounts inside this Chuch magazine.

Above: With my university hopes frustrated, a job had to be found and much would depend on the HSC results. Eddie French and I held long and earnest colloquies about life, the future, girls and the debilitating effect of food rationing in Witton cemetery and Perry playing fields. Perry Hall, seen above, had long been demolished but the moat remained, for use by children's paddle boats.

Right: Does pea pod soup appeal? Food rationing began in January 1940, beginning with butter, sugar and bacon. Meat rationing, by price, followed in March with tea (2 ounces per week) margarine and cooking fats adding to the belt-tightening in the summer.

The KITCHEN FRONT

122 WARTIME RECIPES broadcast by Frederick Grisewood, Mabel Constanduros and others, specially selected by the Ministry of Food.

6 D. NET

Friday 23 August: *Went for a ride round Sutton Park. The park looks lovely with its great sweeps of purple heather.*

I probably turned left, like the car, to cycle into Streetley Lane, along the boundary of the park.

Between the wars, Brummies flocked to Sutton Park especially on fine weather bank holidays. Keepers Pool with its swimming facilities was a popular venue, as the photograph shows. Decorum, for the most part, prevailed.

Monday 26 August: *Market Hall has been burned to the ground. Delayed action bombs in Perry Barr, at the back of the Odeon. Great number of incendiary bombs dropped. Glad Margaret isn't here. Played tennis with Eddie this afternoon. Wrote letters applying for jobs.*

Tuesday 27 August: *Rode up to Jack's but had to make many detours due to unexploded bombs and burst gas and water mains. Continued on to Edna's. Lot of incendiaries down their road* (off Kingstanding Road above).

Left: Thursday 29 August: *Went to see Richard Tauber in 'Land of Smiles'. His singing as always was excellent but it seems such a shame to fit such a talented man to such a poor play and cast.*
This live performance was held at the Theatre Royal. Richard Tauber (1891-1948) an Austrian, was a highly popular tenor, especially in light opera.

Saturday 31 August: *Eventually found Hope & Sons. Willing to set me on. 26s a week – not too bad.* Hours proved to be 8.30 a.m. to 12.30 p.m. and 1.15 p.m. to 5.15 p.m. – an average of forty-two hours a week as alternate Saturday mornings were worked. About three and half mile bicycle ride to the factory and offices of this metal window frames and doors manufacturer.

ON BILBERRY HILL.

The Spirit of Britain

We shall go on to the end.....We shall fight in France, we shall fight on the seas and in the oceans, shall fight with growing confidence and growing strength in the air... We shall defend our island,whatever the cost may be. We shall fight on the beaches,we shall fight on the landing grounds, we shall fight in the fields and streets and in the hills.... We shall never surrender, and even if, which I do not for a moment believe, this island, or even part of it, is subjugated and starving, then our Empire across the seas, armed and guarded by the British Fleet, will carry on the struggle, until, in God's good time, the new world, in all its strength and might, sets forth to the rescue and liberation of the old. Britain will fight the menace of tyranny for years, and, if necessary, alone.

— WINSTON CHURCHILL

Above: After a week's honest and remunerated toil, including Saturday mornings, it was great to ramble around the Lickey Hills with a group of friends from church, all ex-veteran Sunday school attendants. One journey home, interrupted by an air-raid warning, meant that we had to leave the tram. Nothing daunted us, and we pounded the pavements singing cheerfully until eventually 'rescued' by a good old outer circle bus.

Left: Monday 16 September: *Must have been terrific raids on London yesterday, for 185 planes were brought down. A record for the RAF.*
As Churchill said, 'Never in the field of human conflict was so much owed by so many to so few.'

Birmingham Hospital Saturday Convalescent Homes, Romsley Hill Home for Consumptives.

Here's to the doctor

and here's to the nurse
who at any old hour
are never averse
to go to a call and relieve our pain
and put us in fighting fettle again —

**to blast
the hopes
of Hitler !**

"It all depends on ME"

Above: TB remained a constant threat during peace and war. One of the liveliest and merriest lads at HGS, Doug Sandin, was struck down by the disease.

Left: This card is one of a series issued by Ardath Tobacco to emphasise the importance of the civilian contribution to the war effort, in this case the doctors, nurses and ambulance drivers 'ever ready to go out through the blitz and answer the call'.

Opposite: Some of Birmingham's wartime bomb damage can be seen in this picture, unfortunately the exact location is unknown.

Above and below: Saturday 26 October: *Went to the Odeon with Eddie to see Pinnochio, a wonderful production – makes you realise there is something beautiful and creative in the world. Huge glowing fire, engines tearing into town.*

No doubt to help fire engines based at this station in Birmingham (*below*) which opened in 1935.

Saturday 23 November: *Bombs in Church Lane, Oxhill Road, Island Road. Terrible damage. No water or gas.*

If it was a shock when the first outer circle bus trundled past these seventeenth-century cottages in Church Lane, Handsworth, then neighbouring bomb damage must have seemed a desecration.

Wednesday 20 November: *Didn't start work* (in Accounts Department) *until ten, with everyone talking about their crater… becomes a little boring after a time.* Wrong reaction – a bomb exploded on the factory roof that day, *not much damage, save for a lot of broken glass.*

It was probably a desire to hit back that partly prompted my decision to join the Home Guard (Henry Hope Unit). This document (right) was important to self identity and self esteem with the country 'standing alone'.

South Staffordshire Regiment.

This is to Certify that

Eric G. A. Armstrong.

is a Volunteer ~~Officer~~ ~~N.C.O.~~ in the

Smethwick Battalion
Home Guard

HENRY HOPE & SONS LTD

Company.

BATTALION COMMANDER

Drill Hall Smethwick   22/11 1940

"Here's yer kit, an' if there's anything that fits, bring it back an' I'll change it!"

Tuesday 26 November: *Went to the Guard room and obtained tunic, trousers, not serge. All the boots in stock are much too big for my dainty feet – smallest size was a large nine. Anti-gas ointment and field dressings issued.*

Working life settled into a basically agreeable pattern. Paid employment, as a junior clerk, was mildly interesting, and my colleagues were friendly enough. Life outside work became increasingly focussed on the Social Centre at Westminster Road Church, which was built to honour the memory of those who fell in the Great War. Here I would spend evening after evening playing table tennis, snooker and billiards, attending dances and party games; passing the parcel in the cellar during air raids, sharing the company of more girls, especially Jessie, Lois, Joyce and Margaret Tibbetts, Vera and Joan Lamb. Great evenings, and some great daylight hours, rambling.

WARDEN'S REPORT FORM.	A.R.P./M.I.

Form of Report to Report Centres.

(Commence with the words)	"AIR RAID DAMAGE"

Designation of REPORTING AGENT
(e.g., Warden's Sector Number)

POSITION of occurrence

TYPE of bombs :—H.E.   Incendiary   Poison Gas

Approx. No. of CASUALTIES :—
(If any trapped under wreckage, say so)

If FIRE say so :—

Damage to MAINS :—Water   Coal Gas   Overhead electric cables   Sewers

Names of ROADS BLOCKED

Position of any UNEXPLODED BOMBS

Time of occurrence (approx.)

Services already ON THE SPOT or COMING :—

Remarks :—

(Finish with the words)	"MESSAGE ENDS"

ORIGINAL ⎱ These words are for use with a report sent by messenger.
DUPLICATE ⎰ Delete whichever does not apply.

Monday 14 October: *Quite an affectionate letter (from Margaret) seems to be having a good time at the convent… sends me fondest and all her love… motherly advice about air raids.*

Tuesday 15 October: *Had been in bed about an hour when whiz! whiz! whiz! Three bombs came whistling down. Instinctively threw clothes in front of my face in case of flying glass.*

Wednesday 16 October: *Hurried off to Alec. A rattlin' good performance of Ghost Train. Just leaving [the] near exit, [when there were] two shattering detonations, blast blew doors open.*

The 'Alec' was the Alexandra, a city-centre theatre. Until the all clear sounded, an impromptu sing-song was held in the theatre.

Thursday 12 December: *Terrific bang, most probably a land mine as we heard no whistle. Blew one of the windows out. Dashed up to Westminster and Wellington Roads (with mother) to see if everyone was all right. By the lamp-post (in the foreground of the picture) stood a car, its windows open.* With shrapnel pattering down heavily, we leaned into the car to protect our heads, leaving other parts to chance.

Vickers Supermarine S.6B was brilliantly designed and engineered by Rolls Royce to break the world air speed record. This was achieved in 1931 at 407mph. A direct descendant of this plane was the Spitfire which, with the 213 Hawker Hurricane, won the Battle of Britain and lifted the morale of the British people.

THE DART VALLEY SPITFIRE.

THERE'LL ALWAYS·BE·AN· ENGLAND

While British fighters
roam the skies,
The Empire is assured,
That with men like these,
And our sons of the seas,
Her flag will never
be lowered!

Extract from *Modern Wonders*, December 1939: 'The Spitfire, the most deadly of all fighting aircraft. Britain is fortunate in possessing this remarkable machine with which there is none comparable anywhere in the world.'

Around 5,000 Spitfires were built during the Second World War. Like many others, the Dart Valley Spitfire (*above*) is named after the area where local people raised the money to buy it. The two-seater plane was popular because it could attack the enemy with forward fixed machine guns, and was able to fly below enemy aircraft and with its rear gun keep up a continuous fire.

Left: A propaganda card from the early 1940s.

No matter what the heavy odds
You're up against, my friend
Still play the game, whate'er betide
You'll win through in the end

Left: Passing from boyhood into adulthood is not the easiest of transitions, even in peacetime, but in wartime, uncertainties about the future multiply and carry a particular quality of menace. Even so, the mode of conduct urged upon this young cricketer is a good one.

A
BACHELOR'S
SOLILOQUY

To marry
    or not to marry:
That is the question
Whether 'tis better
To remain single
And disappoint
        a few girls —
For a time;
Or wed
And disappoint
        One girl —
For life!

502

Thursday 19 December: *Had a Christmas card from Margaret.*
An impulsive kiss with ... on New Year's Eve set emotions and conscience in a right old tizzy. Oh heck! Volunteer for the Navy? – I had rowing boat experience – or wait to be called up? Que sera, sera.
Separation v Propinquity, an all too familiar wartime dilemma.

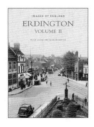

Other Birmingham titles published by Tempus

If you are interested in purchasing other books published by Tempus, or in case you have difficulty finding any Tempus books in your local bookshop, you can also place orders directly through our website

www.tempus-publishing.com

or from   **BOOKPOST**, Freepost, PO Box 29, Douglas, Isle of Man, IM99 1BQ
tel 01624 836000   email bookshop@enterprise.net